Clear and Creative Thinking

Your Key to Working Smarter

Herb Kindler, Ph.D.

A Fifty-Minute™ Series Book

Clear and Creative Thinking

Your Key to Working Smarter

Herb Kindler, Ph.D.

CREDITS:

Senior Editor: **Debbie Woodbury**
Editor: **Ann Gosch**
Assistant Editor: **Genevieve Del Rosario**
Production Manager: **Denise Powers**
Design: **Nicole Phillips**
Production Artist: **Zach Hooker**

ISBN 1-56052-672-6
Library of Congress Catalog Card Number 2002100024
Printed in Canada by Webcom Limited

2 3 4 5 6 PM 06 05 04

Learning Objectives For:

CLEAR AND CREATIVE THINKING

The objectives for *Clear and Creative Thinking* are listed below. They have been developed to guide you, the reader, to the core issues covered in this book.

THE OBJECTIVES OF THIS BOOK ARE:

❏ 1) To explain how clear thinking can open the reader's mind to new ways of looking at problems and opportunities

❏ 2) To explore creative and analytical techniques for generating fresh possibilities

❏ 3) To illustrate the role that values, culture, and goals have in resolving an issue successfully

❏ 4) To help readers understand and select appropriate strategies for implementing decisions

ASSESSING YOUR PROGRESS

In addition to the learning objectives above, Course Technology has developed a Crisp Series **assessment** that covers the fundamental information presented in this book. A 25-item, multiple-choice and true/false questionnaire allows the reader to evaluate his or her comprehension of the subject matter. To buy the assessment and answer key, go to www.courseilt.com and search on the book title or via the assessment format, or call 1-800-442-7477.

Assessments should not be used in any employee selection process.

About the Author

Herb Kindler, Ph.D., is director of Herb Kindler & Associates, a firm that conducts training programs on clear and creative thinking, managing disagreement constructively, stress management, and leadership skill building.

Herb's clients include General Motors, AARP, JVC, Symantec, IBM, Lockheed Martin, TRW, Mattel, UCLA, UC Berkeley, Starbucks, and the U.S. Navy. For program information, contact Herb at P.O. Box 201, Pacific Palisades, CA 90272; telephone (310) 459-0585; e-mail herbkindler@aol.com.

A graduate of MIT, Herb holds a master's degree in public administration; he also has a doctorate in management from UCLA. He was a chief engineer and CEO in industry before becoming professor of management and organization development at Loyola Marymount University in Los Angeles. This is Herb's fifth Crisp Publications book.

Acknowledgments

Special thanks to Marilyn Ginsburg and Ron Jacobs for their helpful, creative, and clear-thinking contributions.

Dedication

This book is dedicated to Peggy, Pat, Debbie, David, and Alex.

Contents

Introduction

Why didn't I think of that!?

Do opportunities escape your attention? Do proposals have unexpected adverse consequences? Do problems go undetected too long? It isn't easy to step outside your own thinking, and even harder to see where your thinking went awry.

That's where clear thinking comes in. Clear and creative thinking precedes effective and compassionate action, advancing what you value. Practicing clear thinking enables you to improve your performance by:

> ➤ Drawing useful conclusions from limited information

> ➤ Tapping your creativity to generate fresh possibilities

> ➤ Translating promising opportunities into desired outcomes

> ➤ Using logic and intuition as allies to anticipate and resolve problems

So what exactly is *clear thinking*? Let's look at this term in relation to others used throughout the book in discussing creative and analytical thinking.

> ➤ Thinking is cognition and emotion that enables you to understand and appreciate the reality you and others perceive

> ➤ Clear thinking minimizes the influence of distorting filters such as mind-sets, attachments, assumptions, and expectations

> ➤ Creative thinking adds value by discovering or inventing new ways of looking at the familiar

> ➤ Critical thinking is the use of analytical reasoning to draw useful conclusions from limited information and to verify the truth of a claim or assertion

Based on hundreds of skill-building workshops, this book offers practical suggestions and helpful exercises for clear, effective thinking. Participating in this book's exercises will help you to make the concepts your own. As you work through the book, you will be learning how to:

➤ Judge the soundness of proposed ideas

➤ Avoid crises

➤ Heighten your awareness of bias

➤ Resolve ethical dilemmas

➤ Communicate in ways that foster empathic understanding

Start now by identifying a real-life issue of concern to you—something about your work, a disagreement, or a career question. Write your issue below. Think about this issue as you work through the book. Some of the exercises will have you referring to this focal issue as you apply clear-thinking concepts toward its resolution.

_____

_____

_____

_____

_____

_____

_____

Opening Your Mind
to Clear Thinking

" *Nothing has such power to broaden the mind as the ability to investigate systematically and truly all that comes under thy observation in everyday life.*"

—Marcus Aurelius, *Meditations*

2

Developing a Whole-Picture Perspective

In a famous quote, Woody Allen once said, "More than at any time in history, mankind is at a crossroads. One path leads to despair and utter hopelessness, the other to total extinction. Let us pray we have the wisdom to choose correctly."

Allen was poking fun at "either/or" ways of thinking—choosing between two undesirable alternatives. But too many people get bogged down in just such a quagmire with seemingly no way out.

Clear thinking helps you to break free of such a limited perspective.

That's because clear thinking skills require looking at the *whole system* in which problems and opportunities occur. Except in the spiritual realm, everything is part of a larger system. By identifying a larger context, you open your mind to multiple possibilities rather than feeling compelled to choose the lesser of two evils.

When you look at the whole system in which problems and opportunities occur, you are receptive to new ways of thinking and responding.

Clear thinking helps you identify hidden assumptions and question unchallenged beliefs. It helps you break free of mind-set conditioning, the ways you have been *conditioned* to respond.

As you review the issue you recorded in the introduction, ask yourself:

> *What is the system or larger picture of which this issue is a part?*

Two tools for whole-picture thinking are incremental and transformational strategies.

Incremental Thinking

Incremental thinking is appropriate when you feel essentially satisfied with the status quo and simply want modest improvements. In an organizational context, incremental thinking is the core of continuous improvement programs. Japanese manufacturers, masters of incremental improvement, call this kind of thinking *kaizen*.

Incremental change is step-by-step movement along the path by which you intend to reach your goals and realize your values. Each step within the current system aims at an improvement in *degree*.

Most people are able to think incrementally as they plan to do more of the same and do it better. Incremental thinking works for dealing with "maze problems," in which step-by-step movement along a path will get you to your goal. It is when incremental changes fail to adequately advance your goals that a shift to transformational thinking is in order. Then it is time to "knock down maze walls" and rebuild.

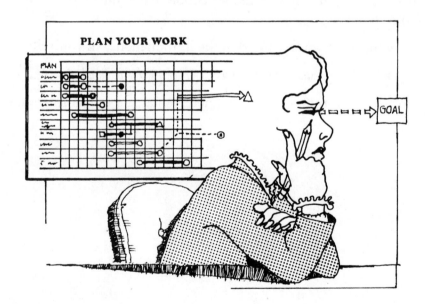

Transformational Thinking

Rather than merely taking incremental steps toward change, transformational thinking involves forming a new concept of the current system. This results in a break in thinking. Transformational thinking is radical in that it changes established procedures. It challenges the assumptions underlying such statements as, "We've always done it this way."

> *Transformational change* is based on a new paradigm, a different way of thinking. It replaces an established framework and aims at renewal rather than refinement. Transformation is a change, not in degree (as in incremental thinking), but in *kind*.

Transformational thinking requires a cognitive leap and the emotional will to risk not knowing what's next. You land in unfamiliar territory. Transformational thinking "breaks the mold."

Management consultants Michael Hammer and James Champy advocate transformational thinking, which they call *reengineering*. "At the heart of business reengineering," they say, "is discontinuous thinking—abandoning outdated rules and assumptions."

Incremental vs. Transformational Thinking

Incremental	Transformational
➤ Works within the current system	➤ Replaces established framework
➤ Step-by-step improvements	➤ A different way of thinking
➤ Changes in degrees	➤ Changes in kind
➤ More of the same, only better	➤ Challenges assumptions
➤ Like working through a maze	➤ Like knocking down walls and rebuilding
➤ Lower risk	➤ Higher risk

CASE STUDY: A LESSON FROM HISTORY

Although the term *transformational thinking* may have been unknown a century ago, it was being practiced, as the following historical example illustrates.

During his 1912 presidential campaign, Theodore Roosevelt planned a train trip to speak with voters and to distribute informative pamphlets. The pamphlet cover presented an impressive photograph of Roosevelt. Unfortunately, no one from Roosevelt's staff noticed—until three million copies were printed—the words under the photo that read: "Moffett Studios, Chicago." Campaign chief George Perkins was horrified to learn that his campaign literature featured unauthorized copyrighted material, and the going rate for reproduced photos was one dollar per copy.

If the copyright holder demanded the full fee, the campaign would be bankrupt and the candidate's financial acumen brought into question. On the other hand, if the copyright issue were ignored, Roosevelt's ethics could be discredited. Instead of "either/or" thinking—choosing between two negatives—Perkins *transformed* a potential catastrophe by looking at the larger picture.

He wired Moffett:

"Planning on giving national publicity to your studios with three million pamphlets bearing your photograph of Theodore Roosevelt. Will you help defray the cost of pamphlet printing?" The publicity idea appealed to the Moffett Studios president who replied: "All I can afford is $250." Perkins accepted.

What might be another way you could have transformed the situation?

_____

_____

_____

TRANSFORM THE PROFIT MARGIN

Try your hand at transformational thinking with the following scenario.

Assume you are CEO of a sporting goods company and you are dissatisfied with profit margins for the baseballs you manufacture. Your profit goal during the coming two-year period cannot be met by *incremental* changes such as lower costs through more efficient use of suppliers, reduced inventory, and altered production sequences.

You need to knock down some "maze walls." What is your thinking about a transformational possibility?

_____

_____

_____

_____

This scenario actually occurred in the Rawlings Sporting Goods Company in 1998. Its thinking was to identify a new sporting goods market that was largely untapped. The company proposed a new product that would monitor the speed of a pitched baseball. This market had been dominated by radar equipment priced between $1,000 and $1,500. Rawlings researchers embedded a microchip processor and liquid crystal display in baseballs to show how fast the balls traveled from the pitching mound to home plate. Priced at less than $40 each, the product was an instant success.

Timing a Strategy Shift

It is one thing to understand the difference between the two whole-picture thinking strategies. But when do you know it is time to change from incremental to transformational thinking? One way is to map the rate of growth of a desired outcome.

For example, you can plot "profits" on a vertical axis and "time" on a horizontal axis. When profits are increasing at a healthy rate, *incremental* improvements are appropriate. All you need are refinements within the present system. Before you reach the point where profit growth tapers off, however, you should be hatching creative ideas for the next *transformational* change.

Although transformation is the more challenging strategy—requiring creativity and a supportive organizational culture—the two thinking strategies are complementary allies as suggested in the diagram below.

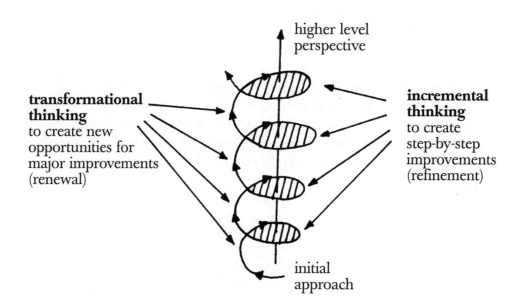

Transformational-Incremental Change Cycle

Combining Reasoning and Emotion

A common misconception holds that clear thinking cannot take place in the presence of emotion. But research now indicates that both cognitive reasoning and emotional involvement are essential for purposeful, effective, and satisfying engagement in life and work.

As neurologist Antonio Damasio concluded: "Certain aspects of emotion and feeling are indispensable for rationality. Feelings point us in the right direction, take us to the appropriate place in decision-making, where we may put the instruments of logic to good use. The emotional brain is as involved in reasoning as is the cognitive brain." He goes on to say: "Reduction in emotion is at least as prejudicial to rationality as excessive emotion."

In other words, when we are flooded or overwhelmed with feelings, rational thinking suffers. But by the same token, when we are not stirred or moved by emotion, we have little impetus to engage our rational minds in pursuing goals.

Daniel Goleman, author of *Emotional Intelligence*, adds: "We have two kinds of intelligence: rational and emotional. The new paradigm urges us to find a balance of the two. . . to harmonize head and heart."

In everyday language, when we ask ourselves: "What do I think about launching this project?" or "What do I think about Pat getting the promotion I expected?" we want integrated answers from both our logical and emotional sides.

Indeed, cognitive reasoning and emotional involvement are complementary skills in clear and creative thinking. It is on this premise that the *Thinking Preference Profile* is built. In the following self-scoring exercise, you will be able to examine your thinking preferences to help you further develop your capacity for clear, creative thinking.

YOUR THINKING PREFERENCE PROFILE

Quantifying your capacity to think clearly and creatively is as difficult as assigning numbers to motivation, morale, or modesty. Nevertheless, this profile questionnaire is designed to stimulate your inquiry into your thinking patterns.

Please respond to the following questions. There are no right or wrong answers. Circle one number for each question using the following key:

4 = almost always   3 = frequently   2 = occasionally   1 = almost never

1. I use logic in reaching conclusions.   4 3 2 1

2. I weigh several factors when thinking about investing (such as my age, budget, future earnings).   4 3 2 1

3. I postpone decision making when I feel out of sorts or tired.   4 3 2 1

4. My approach to relationships: "Are the rewards likely to be worth the effort?"   4 3 2 1

5. I consult my feelings when deciding on a course of action.   4 3 2 1

6. I take the time to get emotionally centered before making important decisions.   4 3 2 1

7. I support my decisions with empirical evidence and reasonably objective facts.   4 3 2 1

8. I avoid arguments likely to generate stressful reactions.   4 3 2 1

9. I approach relationships with an open-hearted desire to connect with another person.   4 3 2 1

10. I decide whether to take an expensive vacation after asking myself if it will add joy to my life.   4 3 2 1

11. I am drawn to people who challenge my intellect.   4 3 2 1

12. When my intuition and logic are in conflict, I rely on logic.   4 3 2 1

CONTINUED

13. I pay close attention when I "know" something "in my bones" or when I experience chills or other body signals for no apparent physiological reason. **4 3 2 1**

14. I reject conclusions of others when they are not supported by facts. **4 3 2 1**

15. I decide whether to take an expensive vacation after asking myself if I can afford it. **4 3 2 1**

16. I get creative ideas from dreams, hunches, or other unexpected sources. **4 3 2 1**

For every term in *both* columns below, insert a number using the following key:

4 = very strong influence on how I <u>behave</u>
3 = strong influence on how I <u>behave</u>
2 = moderate influence on how I <u>behave</u>
1 = negligible influence on how I <u>behave</u>

17. _____ Concepts

18. _____ Empathy

19. _____ Intuition

20. _____ Understanding

21. _____ Facts

22. _____ Compassion

23. _____ Practical

24. _____ Passionate

25. _____ Gut Feelings

26. _____ Emotions

27. _____ Logic

28. _____ Reasoning

29. _____ Appreciating

30. _____ Instincts

31. _____ Objectivity

32. _____ Experimental

33. _____ Analytical

34. _____ Rationality

Scoring

Transfer the numbers you circled and inserted from the previous pages in the appropriate spaces below. Then, add the numbers in each column.
(Note: Numbers do not follow in sequence.)

1. _____	3. _____
2. _____	5. _____
4. _____	6. _____
7. _____	8. _____
11. _____	9. _____
12. _____	10. _____
14. _____	13. _____
15. _____	16. _____
17. _____	26. _____
27. _____	18. _____
28. _____	19. _____
20. _____	29. _____
21. _____	30. _____
31. _____	22. _____
23. _____	32. _____
33. _____	24. _____
34. _____	25. _____
Total _____	**Total** _____
= Cognitive Preference	**= Emotional Preference**

Refer to the chart on the next page to guide you in interpreting your scoring.

Cognitive Reasoning		
	LOW	HIGH
HIGH (Emotional Involvement)	**I** Seeks Precedents and Guidance from Others, Acts Dramatically	**II** Experimental and Creative, Personal and Empathic
LOW (Emotional Involvement)	**III** Seeks Routines, Neglects Searching Inquiry	**IV** Seeks Factual Evidence, Logic and Objectivity, Impersonal

Chart: Cognitive and Emotional Thinking

Scores above 50 reflect an area of highly developed thinking preference.

Scores below 35 suggest an area for further thinking-skill development.

Scores between 35 and 50 reflect an area of moderately developed thinking preference.

The intent of your *Thinking Preference Profile* is to suggest where to focus your energy to further develop your capacity for clear, creative thinking. The parts that follow will guide you in this pursuit.

14

Generating

Alternative Ideas

" *In the beginner's mind there are many possibilities; in the expert's there are few."*

–Suzuki Roshi, *Zen Mind, Beginner's Mind*

Sparking Your Creative Imagination

Creativity breaks existing patterns to clear space for original thinking geared toward achieving valued outcomes. Whether the desired outcome is a product, services, research, humor, advertising copy, a strategic business plan, presentations, or professional and personal relationships, exercising your creativity will help you break free of the usual, standard ways of thinking and move toward new ideas and opportunities.

How can you think in ways that generate creative transformational possibilities? This section will cover five techniques for sparking your creative imagination:

➤ **Constraints**   ➤ **Dramatization**

➤ **"What If" Scenarios**   ➤ **Reframing**

➤ **Dialectic Thinking**

Each of these techniques has its place in the creative process, depending on the problem or issue to be explored. What they all have in common is that they stimulate your imagination to develop new ways of resolving the problem.

Constraints

A constraint imposes *tension* between limitation and possibility that stimulates your imagination to resolve the tension.

Newspaper and magazine writers commonly deal with a space constraint. Initially, writers may insist they cannot be constrained to a specific word count, that they cannot cover the subject in less space. But for seasoned writers, the tension imposed by the space constraint invariably stimulates deeper thought, richer expression, or clearer phrasing as a way of resolving that tension.

Another type of constraint, suggested by Edward de Bono, one of the world's foremost authorities on creative thinking, uses randomly selected words as a creative stimulus. His hypothesis: "Any two inputs cannot remain separate to the human mind. No matter how unconnected, they will establish some sort of link."

Even if you doubt the validity of de Bono's theory, connect a real issue with a randomly chosen word to see if it stimulates fresh, useful ideas. Try the following "Constraints" exercise.

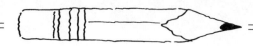

ESTABLISH A LINK

Identify a problem of interest to you using a minimum of words, such as college tuition, car safety, affordable housing, marital intimacy, information overload, career advancement.

Your issue:_____

Open a dictionary and record the 13th word on the opened page. Or, for this exercise, choose one of the following words selected at random: salmon, pliers, microphone, charter, jostle, pelvic, sincere, crown, slither, decipher.

Your word:_____

Let your mind freely connect your issue and the arbitrarily selected word. Without judgment, write your connections in the following spaces.

_____

_____

_____

For example, if my *issue* was "car safety" and my random *word* was "charter," my connections might be:

➤ Charter a bus to pick up and deliver persons too drunk to drive

➤ Charter a citizen's club whose members share the common interest of alerting government officials to post traffic speed signs and install speed bumps

➤ Encourage all students at charter schools to enroll in driver education courses

Just as irritants stimulate an oyster's pearl-producing activity, constraints animate creativity. They open fresh vistas, break worn patterns, and help you escape cliché thinking.

"What If" Questions

The fundamental issue for innovators is adding value. But such a serious intent taps logic more than it stimulates imagination. That's where "what if" questions come in: They open you to playful possibilities. Creativity blossoms in the light of playfulness.

Alex Osborn, co-founder of one of the world's largest ad agencies, suggested that child-like questions give you access to your inherent creativity. Applying logic can come later when it is time to shape the ideas in practical ways that add value.

For now, just consider all the "what if" questions you could ask if you needed to brainstorm new product ideas. Begin by asking, "What if this product were ..." and fill in the blank with these possibilities:

➤ Larger or smaller?

➤ Reversed?

➤ Vocal?

➤ Combined or split?

➤ Illuminated?

➤ Softened or hardened?

➤ Heavier or lighter?

➤ Customized?

➤ Electrified?

➤ Networked?

➤ Insulated?

➤ Liquefied?

➤ Colder or warmer?

➤ More colorful or less colorful?

➤ Looser or tighter?

➤ More fragrant or less fragrant?

➤ Stationary or mobile?

➤ Priced lower or priced higher?

➤ Guaranteed?

➤ Thinner or thicker?

CASE STUDY: NEW PRODUCTS FROM "WHAT IF" QUESTIONS

The following examples show how asking "what if" questions led two major companies to expand their product lines.

Adhesive bandage strips were, for decades, designed to be unobtrusive–presumably to keep others from noticing that wearers had clumsily cut themselves. But Johnson & Johnson started asking *what if* bandages were more colorful and eye-catching? As a result, the company opened a new market with garish colors festooned with cartoon characters. Children loved these bandages and wore them with pride.

Cassette tape players were not easily portable when Sony wanted to expand its market share. A senior manager asked, "*What if* we made these devices much smaller?" He tossed a small block of wood on a table and told a design group, "Make it this size." (He combined *what if* thinking with a *constraint*.) The resultant product incorporated headphones and miniaturized electronics, culminating in the first Walkman® portable stereo.

In what way would you like to improve the way you do business? Brainstorm "what if" questions that would get you thinking in new ways. Write the possibilities below, no matter how trivial or unworkable they might seem right now.

"What if" question: _____

_____

Resulting possibilities: _____

_____

"What if" question: _____

_____

Resulting possibilities: _____

_____

"What if" question: _____

_____

Resulting possibilities: _____

_____

Dialectic Thinking

F. Scott Fitzgerald observed: "The mark of a developed intellect is that it can accommodate two contradictory ideas at the same time." Surely he was speaking about dialectic thinking!

The dictionary describes dialectic thinking as juxtaposing contradictory ideas and seeking to resolve their conflicts. Think of bringing together opposites and overcoming what appear to be irreconcilable differences.

It is in the resolving of the conflicts that creativity happens. Indeed, dialectic thinking turns rationality on its head! To integrate opposites requires moving from linear logic (sequential reasoning) to more creative thinking.

Dialectic thinking involves three steps:

1. A premise is presented: the thesis

2. An opposing premise is identified: the antithesis

3. The effort to reconcile both premises—the synthesis—stimulates creative ideas

Articulating and working through these three steps forces you to give adequate thought to alternative ideas. Otherwise, it is too easy to compromise too quickly. To embrace both the belief you hold (the synthesis) and its opposite (the antithesis), you have to break your current mind-set. And doing that is what often ignites unexpected insights.

The dialectic thinking tool makes your assumptions explicit. Then you and others can openly judge the soundness of your conclusions. Now exercise your dialectic thinking skills in the following scenario to check your conclusions and explore new ideas.

MOTIVATING EMPLOYEES

A corporate president considers launching an awards banquet to recognize outstanding performers. She asks your opinion about initiating such an annual event.

Let's examine this request using the step-by-step dialectic thinking tool. The first step is presenting the *thesis*: A public awards ceremony, particularly involving financial incentives, will help motivate employees to be more productive.

The second step is identifying the *antithesis*: Changing our own behavior is exceedingly difficult; hoping to change the performance behavior of others is at best a temporary fix.

The third step is reconciling both these premises to develop the *synthesis*. Write below your synthesis that integrates the intent of the president's thesis with the difficulty identified in the antithesis.

Author's suggestions:

Possible synthesis: Everyone is innately motivated. The challenge is not to design events to motivate others but to create environments that support individuals and teams in doing their best work.

Reflecting on this synthesis stimulates these new ideas and possibilities:

➤ Initiating a corporate fellowship or sabbatical program is likely to support motivation. Such a program would offer outstanding performers the opportunity to lead challenging projects of their own choosing for a specific time period with adequate resources.

➤ A team could take an idea they developed and be supported in creating a new enterprise in which these innovative performers and the company would jointly retain stock options.

Dramatization

From the time we were children, we have engaged in role-playing in one form or another, and it is a common teaching tool in adult training seminars. Dramatization is a form of role-playing developed by Jacob Moreno, widely recognized as the father of psychodrama.

Dramatization gives a "voice" to each element of a problem or potential opportunity as individuals play the parts of people and inanimate objects. The role-playing draws out perspectives that might be missed in standard impersonal analysis.

What makes dramatization more than just playing around?

> ➤ Using role-playing to generate alternatives moves beyond *ideation* into the practical arena of *doing*. For example, if you think an apology is appropriate, acting out the apologizing to a real person is a skill-building experience. Role-playing narrows the gap between a hypothetical situation and a real-life interaction.

> ➤ Role-playing offers direct, immediate feedback. It brings into play not just *mental* reactions, but also how others *feel* about how you interact with them. Role-playing is a learning vehicle for emotional skills.

> ➤ Dramatization presents multiple perspectives that often trigger fresh thinking.

CASE STUDY: ELEVATOR BLUES

A newly renovated 20-story office building was quickly leased in downtown Philadelphia. But as the building filled, complaints mounted. People were annoyed waiting in the lobby for elevators. The cost of constructing new elevator shafts was prohibitive. What to do?

A problem-solving meeting using *dramatization* was convened with three role players—a typical person waiting in the lobby, the "lobby" itself, and an "elevator." Here's the dialogue the role-players improvised.

Elevator: *"What's all the fuss? I knock myself out picking up passengers. I don't take breaks. Instead of appreciation, people spill coffee on my new floor. And does everyone have to arrive during the same peak hours?"*

Passenger: *"What if some of you elevators were to stop only on alternate floors? That way you would cut your travel time, and we could easily walk down one flight of stairs."*

Elevator: *"That's not fair to handicapped people."*

Lobby: *"I'm disgusted with this conversation. Why don't you just come out and say it—you hate me. People want to get away from me as fast as they can."*

Passenger: *"You are rather drab. Can't you spruce up your appearance"?*

Lobby: *"Yes. New carpeting would help. How about piping in music? A fish tank would add to my environment."*

Elevator: *"I've got it! Let's install large mirrors in the lobby."*

The dialogue could continue, but you get the idea. From the day the mirrors were actually installed in the lobby, no complaints about elevator delays were ever voiced again.

DRAMATIZE YOUR PROBLEM

Now it is your turn. Using a real problem or concern, identify involved people and relevant objects. Invite co-workers or friends to play certain roles. Do not rehearse; creativity is stimulated by spontaneity. Encourage the players to bounce off one another's dialogue.

The problem I will dramatize: _____

_____

_____

_____

The roles to be played out (individuals or objects): _____

_____

_____

_____

_____

Reframing

Another tool for stimulating creative possibilities is to reframe conventional wisdom by asking yourself: "If I didn't accept the view of reality imposed by others, how else could I define it?" In other words, how could I look at the problem a different way than the way others would have me look at it?

A photo snapshot includes both what is recorded on film and how the photographer framed the picture. Likewise, reality for people is not the actual truth detached from any context. It is the understanding in the minds and hearts of those who are perceiving.

The same round of golf, for example, has a different reality to the professional player than to the caddy. As another example, you may give your employee a gift certificate to a fine restaurant because you value his contributions to the team. But he may reframe your gift giving as an attempt to "butter him up" to work overtime in the coming weeks.

The following historical example illustrates how, through reframing, a different reality was created–more in harmony with your goals and values.

> A French army commander received orders to quell riots in Paris before the 1789 Revolution. He was directed to disperse crowds by shooting unarmed protesters if necessary. As his soldiers leveled their rifles, the commander shouted to an angry crowd: "Mesdames et monsieurs, I have orders to fire at the rabble (*canaille*). But, as I see a great number of honest, respectable citizens before me, I request that these citizens leave so I can safely shoot the rabble." The square emptied in a few minutes.

Reframing also connects with incremental and transformational thinking. For example, in the historical scenario above, opposing hostility with greater hostility would have been *incremental* reasoning–more of the same. Instead, the army commander *transformed* the situation, opening up the possibility for a new solution to emerge.

By reframing the problem at hand, you open your mind to a new solution more in tune with your goals, values, and capabilities.

Tapping into Your Inner Wisdom

Inner wisdom works at a level below the conscious mind. This inner knowing expresses itself as thoughts and feelings (intuition), body sensations (focusing), and dream symbols. In general, relaxation, minimal distraction, released expectations, and a nonjudgmental attitude all help you tap into your inner wisdom.

Intuition

Surely you can recall times when an unexpected insight darted into your awareness, hinting at a direction for you to take. Or, conversely, perhaps you remember when you blamed yourself with: "I *knew* I shouldn't have done that; I ran right through the warning signals." That direct, immediate, holistic inner wisdom is what we identify as intuitive capacity. Everyone has it.

Consider the case of a CEO, who discounted her intuition about an open executive-level position. One candidate, Tom, looked promising on paper and was articulate at the job interview. Even though a little intuitive voice told the CEO that Tom wasn't a leader, logic convinced her otherwise. After all, what better evidence of leadership was there than Tom's serving as an army major? But the CEO's gut turned out to be better attuned than her brain. Fortunately, in time, she found a mutually satisfying match by transferring Tom to a technical staff position.

Although intuition may be on target, its validity cannot be proved definitively. In the example of Tom's inadequate leadership, other factors may have influenced his poor performance at the new job. Perhaps the CEO didn't provide enough training or support, or maybe Tom got depressed listening to his family's unrelenting complaints about being uprooted to another city.

Still, intuition is a powerful tool that stimulates creative possibilities. Your intuitive sense can give you clues to examine and directions to explore.

Getting into a state of gentle receptivity will help you attune to the guidance your intuition offers. Quiet your everyday mind-chatter with deep relaxation. Allow yourself to "let go" and be attentive to your subtle intuitive voice.

Focusing

Developed by University of Chicago psychologist, philosopher, and author Eugene Gendlin, *focusing* is an effective tool for eliciting inner wisdom that might otherwise be inaccessible. The technique depends on being sensitive to subtle body-feeling messages.

Here's an abbreviated scenario adapted from Gendlin's book, *Focusing*, to illustrate how focusing works.

Fred, a sales executive, feels a constant tightness in his stomach (his body-feeling message). Company sales have been declining and Fred's reorganization plan was turned down by his manager. Fred believes his boss doesn't respect him or his ideas.

Take Fred's role, or any problem you are facing, and experiment with the following focusing steps:

1. **Clear your mind.** See what comes into your consciousness when you ask: How am I feeling right now? What about this issue keeps me from feeling wonderful? What else? Anything else?

2. **Sense the totality.** Ask: What does the whole situation or problem feel like? Screen out demeaning self-lectures. Focus on the single feeling that most touches everything that seems awry or off.

3. **Identify a label or handle.** See if you can find words that get to the heart of the problem–words that tell you: "Yes! That's what it is all about."

4. **Check your label.** Is this really the crux of the issue? If it is, you will sense a release (in Fred's case, a release of the knots in his stomach). If not, consider another round.

Let's see how sales manager Fred might have dealt with his issue at each step in the focusing process.

> Fred is worried about his career and angry with his boss. He is also angry with himself for not presenting his plan with more compelling logic. As Fred probes more deeply, he feels a lack of self-confidence and chooses the label "insecure." The knots in his stomach seem to be related to sadness, covered over by anger, that at his age, work is still such a struggle, and he feels so vulnerable.

Focusing helps you direct your attention to identifying what really matters and understanding what needs to be addressed.

Dream Processing

The expression, "Let's sleep on it," reflects the nocturnal process that reorganizes information in ways that can be illuminating. Thus, *dream processing* involves decoding symbolic information found in your dreams and nightmares.

Nobel prize physicist Niels Bohr, after dreaming of horses racing within marked lanes, suddenly grasped what was to be his basic thesis of atomic structure: Electrons must remain in fixed orbits around the nuclei of atoms.

Inventor Elias Howe, stymied and frustrated with his inadequate design for a sewing machine, had a dream. Cannibals captured and started boiling him in preparation for dinner. Each time he tried to escape from the bubbling cauldron, the natives poked him back with sharp spears—each oddly fashioned with a hole near the point. Howe awoke in a sweat with a rush of insight. He "knew" that the thread transport needle of his sewing machine needed a pierced hole not at the blunt end—where it was located during centuries of hand sewing—but at the sharp point. The sewing machine needle was born!

Dreams often have multiple messages. Howe, for example, could have felt sharp prodding because he was in "hot water" with investors—which, indeed, was the case.

Einstein dramatized the power of dreams for problem solving when he said that his entire scientific career was a meditation on his dream of sledding down a hill under a star-filled sky, gaining momentum until he reached the speed of light.

Research concludes that everyone, unless sedated with pills or alcohol, experiences the rapid eye movement that accompanies dreaming. About 20% of total sleep time every night is spent in a dream state. This adds up to four years of the average person's life span.

To gain insights from dreaming, the first challenge is remembering. Try the following strategies:

> ➤ Set the intention to recall your dreams

> ➤ Just before falling asleep, program your unconscious with a specific issue for it to tackle

> ➤ Place pen and paper or a recording device at your bedside

Dreaming is particularly effective in breaking new ground because dreams do not heed cultural constraints or any need to be logical. You are free to be creative without concern for propriety or worry about looking ridiculous.

Using Analytical Reasoning

Analytical reasoning is a useful tool for checking the validity of tentative conclusions and stimulating further creative thinking. Also called critical thinking, it uses inductive and deductive reasoning to draw useful conclusions from limited information.

Before examining everyday, practical, ambiguous issues that permeate our work and personal lives, let's look at the rare problem that has only one correct solution.

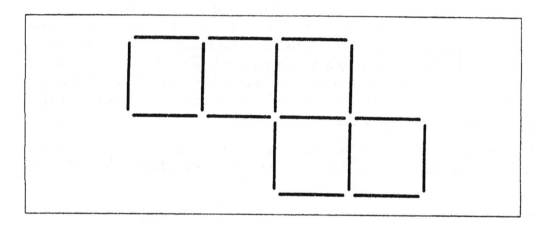

This diagram shows five equal squares made by laying out matchsticks of equal length. Your task is to move just two sticks to new locations and reduce the number of squares from five to four, each the same size as the original squares. Use all matchsticks as sides of squares. Do not discard any sticks or place any on top of or next to other matchsticks. This problem will be solved when—by moving only two sticks—you have constructed four squares using all matchsticks as sides of complete squares.

Try it! You may attempt a trial-and-error approach, but it is rarely successful. Instead, creative imagination and analytical reasoning are the dual partners that will release you from this puzzle's perceptual trap.

Tap into your intuition, a function of your creative imagination, for this clue: Count the sticks—16. Logical analysis, then, should trigger your solution strategy. To use the 16 sticks in just four squares, all four squares must be freestanding. That is, they can touch each other only at the corners.

Try the four-freestanding-squares strategy before checking the key at the end of this book. Which two sticks must be moved?

Inductive Reasoning

When examining all data would be impossible or impractical, *inductive reasoning* leads to a generalized conclusion from particular instances. You start with evidence about *some* members of a class or category. This becomes the basis for your conclusion or theory about *all* members of that class.

Because extrapolating from a limited sample to reach a general conclusion involves uncertainty, inductive reasoning generates only hypotheses or working assumptions. If additional information continues to support your predicted pattern, it strengthens the hypothesis. But even one well-founded contradiction suggests the need to modify or develop a new theory. The march of science is recorded in the rejection of one theory (such as assuming electricity to be a fluid) and the creation of another that better explains new evidence.

People with a vested interest in theories-in-vogue may intentionally avoid disconfirming evidence. A 17th-century example was the refusal of clerics to look through Galileo's new telescope because it might reveal the truth that the earth is not the center of our solar system.

Example of Inductive Reasoning

In the organizational world, an inductive claim could be: Because managers Mario, Susan, and Dao have private offices, it follows that all managers in similar positions have private offices.

Because the reasoning moves to a generalization about all managers, the conclusion has been reached inductively. The evidence—three managers have private offices—contributes to a level of probability that the hypothesis is true. With each new supporting fact, the conclusion gains credibility. But even one valid contradictory case can refute a generalization. Thus, in this example it would be advisable to check the work area of more than three managers before making a claim about all managers.

To evaluate the credibility of any conclusion drawn using inductive reasoning, consider:

Sample Size—The larger the number of people or events studied, the more confidence you will have in the conclusion. Adequate sample size can be determined statistically.

Selection Criteria—Are the people or events *representative* of the whole class under study? Were they chosen *randomly*? Does the sample have the same *mix proportions* as the population under study regarding relevant variables such as gender, race, income level, health, locale, and education?

Researcher Bias—Are the researchers likely to be influenced in favor of or in opposition to a particular outcome? Has relevant information been ignored or discounted? Does the physical presence of the researchers distort what they are observing?

Cause-Effect Relationship—The possibility of a relationship masquerading as causal is an important aspect of critical thinking. Explore the likelihood of a particular event *causing* an observed result.

For example:

➤ *Does shoe size predict intelligence?* Very low probability

➤ *Does the content of your refrigerator predict stress level?* Low probability

➤ *Does a bolt of lightning cause the thunder that follows some seconds later?* Very high probability (experimental evidence confirms that lightning heats the air through which it passes, creating a sudden expansion that generates sound waves).

Even a strong correlation does not ensure a causal link. A fascinating and amusing study once found support for the claim that babies were brought to mothers by storks—at least Swedish babies. A correlation of 0.9 (about as close to a perfect 1.0 as is feasible) was shown to exist over a period of years between the number of stork nests in Stockholm and babies born there! As noted earlier, inductive reasoning generates only hypotheses!

Deductive Reasoning

Just the opposite of induction, *deduction* takes a general statement that makes a claim and applies it to one or more specific situations, events, or people. The purpose of deductive reasoning is to draw reasonable inferences from available information.

Example of Deductive Reasoning

Because all managers have private offices, it follows that Pablo, newly promoted to a managerial position, should be assigned a private office.

A good way to identify deductive reasoning is to note movement from *general* to *specific*—in the example, from "all managers" to "Pablo."

When considering the validity of deductive logic, explore the likelihood that the general principle or policy under consideration helps create a sound basis for future decisions that will be based on it.

For example, in considering managerial work areas, do some managers need privacy while others need to better interface with production? How does the policy affect use of home offices? Does the policy send a signal that the more responsibility you gain in this organization, the more cloistered or aloof you are expected to become?

EVALUATE THE POLICY DECISION

You have been asked to serve on a committee to make recommendations that will improve the quality of newly hired employees. Your committee reaches the following conclusion: All job candidates should be evaluated on how well they match the attitudes and skills of the organization's most effective employees.

The committee believes this policy will result in better performance and less turnover. In your judgment, is this policy recommendation sound and likely to serve corporate needs? Why or why not?

_____

_____

Author's suggestions:

Using deductive reasoning—moving from a general statement to its specific application—let's examine whether the recommended policy is appropriate to the situation.

Proposal Strengths

➤ The organization would review patterns, perhaps for the first time, that contribute to effective job performance

➤ Teamwork might be fostered among employees who have similar attitudes

Proposal Weaknesses

➤ This type of screening might unfairly discriminate and might even lead to litigation by rejected job applicants

➤ Workforce homogeneity might generate minimal disagreement, but fail to spark the creative ideas that emerge when people with diverse backgrounds respectfully confront one another

➤ Employees who currently are most productive might not be the best role models if circumstances were to change radically

We could take an either/or or accept/reject approach to this committee's findings, but a more productive position would be to consider what aspects of the study have merit. For example, the committee's recommendations might not serve corporate hiring needs in their present form. But compiling a list of effective attitudes and skills, periodically updated, could be useful in designing employee training programs.

Understanding Systems Thinking

A special type of thinking helps you understand how purposeful systems function. *Systems thinking* helps you focus on dynamic wholes and how components interact. Then when problems occur you can *change the thinking* that caused the problems in the first place. Again, as in the previous sections, the aim is to generate alternatives.

Clearly, systems thinking is helpful to engineers designing manufacturing plants for pharmaceuticals, power generation, or water purification. But some appreciation of systems thinking is helpful to anyone with organizational responsibilities.

The actions you take, such as outsourcing subassemblies or initiating new procedures, are never isolated. When you change one variable, you effect a change elsewhere in the system. Such changes will not always be apparent to you because they might be local or distant, immediate or delayed.

The following terms are useful in understanding how systems function to improve performance of individuals, teams, and organizations.

> **System.** A network of interacting elements that work together to carry out an objective, purpose, or intention

> **Input.** People—with their ideas, reasoning skills and talents—plus money, material, equipment, information, work space, and such environmental resources as clean air, water, the Internet, roads, and power

> **Processing Capacity.** The system's ability to transform inputs to desired products, services, and knowledge

> **Output.** What the system delivers that becomes the input to other systems or that is recycled to the environment

> **Feedback.** Information about how well outputs match intentions

> **Control.** The system's ability to sense deviations from desired output and to act on this feedback to minimize such digressions.

To see how these system elements function and how they could affect your responsibilities, consider the following case study.

CASE STUDY: SERVING THE CUSTOMER

At Cosmo Electronics, sales drifted steadily lower during the past year. Happily, this quarter, sales are rebounding. Marketing vice president Mark attributes the turnaround to advertising and his new program of financial incentives for sales personnel. To sustain recent rising sales, Mark asked marketing analyst Ann to check future purchase plans of Cosmo's best customers. Ann discovered widespread discontent with late deliveries and inconsistent quality. Some annoyed customers had already placed orders with Cosmo's competitors. Mark responded by naming Ann to the new position of customer services coordinator. Employee reaction (during private water-cooler conversations) was: "Here we go again."

If you were a consultant to Cosmo Electronics' president, what counsel would you offer? Why?

_____

_____

_____

_____

_____

_____

_____

_____

CONTINUED

To gain perspective, let's examine system elements relevant to this case.

➤ **Input.** For Cosmo Electronics, relevant inputs are customer orders, staff skills, raw materials, and financial investment. Management failed to learn why—over a 12-month period—orders had been declining. They should have been asking: How much was due to an economic downturn, how much to customer dissatisfaction, how much to inadequate promotion?

➤ **Processing capacity.** This was Cosmo's most critical system element. Before investing in advertising and offering financial incentives to sales personnel, management needed to ensure the system had adequate capacity to process orders with consistent quality, timely delivery, and first-rate customer support. Salespeople quoting unrealistic delivery dates and unrealistic special-design options to gain sales-incentive rewards could have further exacerbated the company's problems.

➤ **Output, feedback, and control.** Feedback relates desired output to actual output so that appropriate control can ensure on-target processing. But honest feedback can be gained only by building trust and minimizing employee vulnerability. When Cosmo personnel said "Here we go again" only privately, they deprived management of the thinking of those most knowledgeable about what is awry in the system. If incentives are used, they should be based on profits, not sales, and should cover all employees whose feedback counts. Otherwise, insights are lost, energy is withdrawn, and employee focus shifts to self-protection.

Systems Thinking Lessons

The previous customer service case study illustrates the importance of thinking with a whole-picture perspective, covered in Part 1, and of considering the interaction among system components to generate alternative solutions. Review the following lessons about systems thinking:

Systems vs. Linear Thinking. Addressing a problem with sequential, straightline thinking, such as "Sales are down; promote sales," is likely to engender future concerns more challenging than the short-term dilemma it solves.

Collaborative Inquiry. Systems problems are most productively addressed in dialogue with people of diverse perspectives, no matter what their organizational position—including key customers and suppliers. Aim at uncovering any unintended consequences of implementing current thinking.

Introspection. When problems that affect you escalate or recur ("Here we go again"), assume *you* are part of the problem.

Sharing Perspectives with Others

Thomas Jefferson once observed: "Too many are afflicted with impatience for any logic that is not their own." But sharing perspectives with others can enrich clear thinking of the issue and potential alternatives. The idea is not to debate; thinking with others is mutual inquiry, a conversation, a dialogue without ego. The goal is to bring together multiple viewpoints into a coherent whole.

Multiple views are helpful when participants:

➤ Have a common intention and understanding of the issue or problem to be addressed

➤ Think independently about feasible solutions before sharing ideas

➤ Trust and respect one another—so that each contribution is expressed without a hidden agenda

➤ Seek the best thinking without creating a competitive win/lose environment

➤ Do not get attached to or identified with specific outcomes, but instead, remain open to fresh ideas

Dialogue is a strategy for thinking together creatively. It requires remaining curious, tuning in to your inner wisdom and the wisdom of others, and staying open to possibility. The assumption throughout the dialogue should be that each person possesses some insight and that bringing these together will allow a fuller picture to be revealed.

Dialogue for Organization Development

Group dialogue gained acceptance as an organization development tool at the end of World War II with the advent of two communication laboratory experiments—Tavistock Study Group in England and National Training Laboratory (NTL) in the United States. The programs were called T-groups, sensitivity training, and laboratory learning. Initially they were aimed at business executives interested in leadership and personal growth. At the training labs, participants typically spent 10 days together in an isolated setting without much structure or a preplanned agenda. Their central message remains applicable today:

> ➤ If you speak candidly without equivocation and if you take responsibility for the consequences of choices you make, you will be a more effective leader

> ➤ Thinking with others depends on gaining an understanding of how your behavior is seen by them

> ➤ What you learn in the laboratory will flow primarily from experiences you share with other participants

Charles Handy, professor at the London School of Business, tells of his experience at one of the early NTL programs in the United States.

> I was nervous, apprehensive, and on my best behavior—concealing my alarm to learn that the entire first week would be unstructured—no agenda, no leader, no timetable. I was an outsider from abroad and decided to keep quiet and watch the others discuss a plan. At one point, someone suggested that we check impressions. This was the instruction:

> "Put your name on a piece of paper and pass it around. We each will write a word or phrase describing how we see you. When all the papers have gone around, we will each unfold our own and find the comments."

> I had nothing to lose. I had said nothing and expected to get back an empty sheet of paper. But I had a full complement of comments: "Snob, Patronizing, Stuck Up, Unapproachable, Superior," and more. I realized they had dumped all their stereotypes of the British onto me. I jumped to my feet, red-faced and furious, stung into speech ending with: " ... and, I'm not even British. I'm Irish." They laughed. I forgave them. It was me speaking, not a silent stereotype.

Notice how people tend to project onto others impressions based on experience and expectation. Note also how forgiving and cooperative people are when you reveal who you really are and allow yourself to be vulnerable.

Four Principles for Group Dialogue

Encouraging people to feel safe enough to be candid is a leadership challenge. Creating an environment that supports authenticity brings out the most productive thinking because people say what they know and how they feel. They don't feel the need to hide behind roles. Follow these operating principles to help promote a productive group dialogue:

Clarify Ground Rules and a Common Purpose

When you convene a dialogue group, identify common interests worthy of the considerable time required to think together effectively. The purpose may be strategic issues at work, or issues that concern everyone such as:

> ➤ How can we create an environment that better supports personal and professional renewal?

> ➤ What assumptions are we making that limit performance and satisfaction?

Be Fully Present to Your Direct Experience

Presence requires sensitive self-awareness and attuning to what is happening in the moment. You detract from your presence when you try to impress others; avoid feelings, including your own; and rush to fill what you perceive to be an awkward silence.

Ask yourself, Do I allow myself to say what's true for me:

> ➤ Without concern for what impression I am making?

> ➤ Without feeling the need for mental rehearsing?

> ➤ Without assurance from others that I am "right"?

Listen with a "Third Ear"

Consider the advice of management pioneer Elton Mayo: "Listen to what others want to say, listen to what they do not want to say, and listen to what they cannot say without support."

Don't distract yourself with expectation, judgment, or thinking about a rebuttal. Listen with the attitude that you don't have to prepare any response. When you listen with the sole intent of understanding what is and isn't being said, you non-verbally communicate respect for the speaker, respect that paves the way for productive collaboration.

See Yourself in the Experience of Others

As much as you are willing to expose your vulnerabilities, others are likely to see some of their own issues in your experience. And, when others speak, their experience may serve as a mirror to reflect and clarify your own issues and creative possibilities.

GATHER THE GROUP'S INSIGHTS

Answer the following questions to identify how you would apply the four operating principles for group dialogue to a real issue on which you want to gain further insight.

Who else is involved in the issue and should be invited to participate in thinking together?

_____

_____

What is the common purpose that will motivate participants' desire to draw out the group's best thinking?

_____

_____

What ground rules will you want to adopt to ensure disclosure of sensitive information?

_____

_____

_____

What traps do you need to avoid? Bias based on parochial interests? Desire to "look good"? Fear of uncertainty? List the traps that apply to your situation.

_____

_____

_____

How can you create a safe meeting environment, free of distraction, that supports participants in listening to each other with full attention?

_____

_____

_____

Evaluating Alternatives on Their Merits

"Whenever I have to choose between two evils, I always like to pick the one I haven't tried before."

—Mae West

The "Six Lens" Approach

The previous part covered generating alternative ideas through creativity, reasoning, and group dialogue. But moving from idea to implementation, in almost all organizations, takes place through proposals. So once you have an action plan in mind or on paper, how do you evaluate its merit for your organization?

Let's say a colleague plops a draft proposal on your desk or in your e-mail with the request, "Let me have your thoughts on this." Would you have an effective, systematic, credible game plan for developing an appropriate response?

This is where the "Six Lens" approach comes in. At the heart of every proposal are six basic values:

> **Technical**

> **Economic**

> **Ethical-legal**

> **Environmental**

> **Power-political**

> **Social-psychological**

The Six Lenses guide you in your response—whether to recommend implementing, rejecting, or modifying the proposal. Collectively, these lenses clarify how well a proposal aligns your organization's goals, culture, and values. Let's focus on each of these lenses in more detail.

Technical Lens

> The **technical** lens examines the capacity of a proposed action to determine if it can effectively accomplish the task for which it was designed. Focus: *Can it do the job?*

To judge the technical merit of a proposed course of action, you could consult technical specialists such as engineers, scientists, software developers, and other professionals.

For example, suppose your goal involves a complex technology such as the use of a nonpolluting, renewable fuel to power cars. Assume project managers in your company propose developing fuel cells that convert methanol to hydrogen. Hydrogen would combine with oxygen in a chemical reaction that would generate enough electricity to propel a car. Rather than pollutants that spew from conventional tailpipes, fuel-cell-powered cars would emit harmless water, carbon dioxide, and some heat.

In this example, concerns to examine under a *technical* lens would include:

- ➤ Hydrogen safety

- ➤ Car handling

- ➤ Acceleration

- ➤ Warm-up time

- ➤ Driving range

- ➤ Maintenance requirements

- ➤ Noise

- ➤ Methanol availability

- ➤ Space required for the on-board "refinery"

If the technical analysis were encouraging, then a performance comparison with other alternative technologies, such as hybrid gasoline-battery cars, would be prudent.

The technical lens need not be limited to complex technologies. It can be used to study modest change proposals such as a purchasing procedure or a new method for packing sardines. Take this homey story about the technology of soap making.

> When Tom, a college student, stopped to fix a flat tire in front of a small, rural soap-making factory, he started talking with the factory owner. During the conversation, Tom decided on-the-spot to become a soap salesman. Soap rationing had just ended along with World War II. Tom sold out his first carload of soap so quickly that he began thinking about franchising regional territories. He decided to start by soliciting testimonials from his customers and returned to the wife of one of his professors. Rather than praising the soap, however, she held out her bright red hands and asked, "Is this normal?" At that moment, Tom didn't need a special lens to see that finishing college would be more rewarding than owning franchise rights to this less-than-ideal soap-making technology.

Now consider the real-life issue you identified in the introduction and describe any technical concerns you might have:

_____

_____

How can you address these concerns using means that are feasible and effective so your intention will come to pass?

_____

_____

_____

Economic Lens

> The **economic** lens looks at a proposed investment—money, material, time, people, and other resources—to determine the probability of recovering the investment and earning a return commensurate with the risks.
> Focus: *Will it pay?*

The economic lens evaluates the probability of reaching a desired financial goal when the outcome is not predictable. A risk-taking analysis is helpful whether you have organizational responsibilities—such as improving productivity, leveraging intellectual property, expanding market share—or you are handling personal finances—planning for college, buying long-term care insurance, refinancing your home, investing for retirement.

Four elements deserve your attention in considering any investment: potential for gain, exposure to loss, level of uncertainty, and your subjective risk-taking tendency. Work through the following exercise to help you understand each element.

Potential for Gain

Write a concise statement of what you hope to gain from a specific investment—of time, energy, money and other resources.

_____

_____

_____

_____

_____

Exposure to Loss

How might you lose more of your—or your corporation's—investment than you are willing to tolerate? Explore means of reducing your vulnerability to excessive loss. For example, for personal funds, does it make sense to buy insurance, place stop-loss orders on stocks you own, diversify your portfolio, or use other investment instruments? Organizations seeking to reduce vulnerability to loss might test new ideas with prototypes or computer simulations, conduct random audits, develop worst-case scenarios, hedge overseas currencies, or form alliances. Write your plan below.

_____

_____

_____

_____

_____

Level of Uncertainty

Contrary to the image of a manager as a quick-on-the-draw gunslinger, some uncertainty often can be dispelled by delaying a decision as long as feasible. Use available time to consult multiple, independent sources. Debt repayment, for example, can be made more certain by running a credit check, requiring collateral, or securing a bank letter-of-credit. What ideas can you think of for reducing uncertainty about a specific issue you are exploring?

_____

_____

_____

_____

_____

Your Risk-Taking Bias

Evaluate your personal orientation to risk seeking and risk-aversion. Research suggests that individuals in each orientation tend to display similar characteristics as outlined below.

Risk seekers tend to:	Risk avoiders tend to:
Underrate uncertainties	Overrate uncertainties
Be overly optimistic	Be overly pessimistic
Enjoy the excitement of the unknown	Prefer comfort and security
Overrate or exaggerate probability of realizing desired outcomes	Underrate or ignore probability of realizing desired outcomes
Decide impulsively	Postpone decision-making or close the opportunity door too quickly
Motto: *Nothing ventured, nothing gained*	Motto: *Better safe than sorry*

The key is to be aware of a significant bias because you may be either inflating or underestimating potential gains, losses, and uncertainties. You may recognize that a preference for either stimulation or security motivates your risk-taking decisions. Some people thrive on excitement and change; others prefer calm and stability. A strong preference for stimulation may propel people to sky dive, watch scary movies, or travel on impulse to exotic places. A strong leaning toward security may lend itself to establishing routines, preferring closure to ambiguity, and seeking comfort in what is familiar.

Risk-Taking Continuum

Think about your own tendency toward risk seeking and risk avoidance. Where do you fall on the continuum?

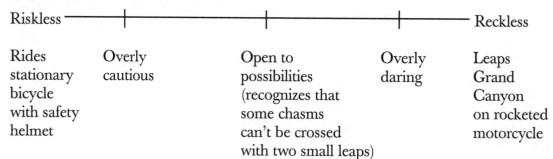

Riskless			Reckless
Rides stationary bicycle with safety helmet	Overly cautious	Open to possibilities (recognizes that some chasms can't be crossed with two small leaps)	Overly daring · Leaps Grand Canyon on rocketed motorcycle

Ethical-Legal Lens

> The **ethical-legal** lens examines a proposal's compliance with applicable law. Ethical behavior is more inclusive. It looks at the well-being of individuals, the needs of groups and of societal systems vulnerable to the consequences of a proposed action. Focus: *Is this the "right" thing to be doing?*

Ethical behavior requires a higher standard than simply complying with the law. The ethical-legal lens helps you decide, for example, if it is appropriate to hire detectives to rummage through a competitor's garbage. Such an activity is not illegal (if the detectives don't trespass), but their ethics might be questionable.

The work of Lawrence Kohlberg, who for many years directed Harvard University's Center for Moral Development, provides a comprehensive overview of the ethical criteria.

> Following Kohlberg's maritime experience in World War II, he volunteered to transport homeless Holocaust survivors to Palestine. England governed Palestine and passed a law prohibiting immigration of displaced Jews into this territory. During Kohlberg's first sea voyage with "smuggled" refugees, their ship was rammed by a British warship and boarded by sailors firing tear gas and clubbing passengers who resisted them. Kohlberg was shocked by the incident and appalled to learn that the British later imprisoned the passengers on Crete.

> Kohlberg wondered: Was he morally justified to violate British law? Is violating any law justified because you object to its fundamental premise?

Three-Level Reasoning

After decades of study, Kohlberg concluded that ethical reasoning involves choosing among three levels:

> ➤ Self-interest

> ➤ System Maintenance

> ➤ Principled Behavior

Each succeeding level reflects a higher degree of ethical conduct. Viewing a moral dilemma through this three-level lens can guide your inquiry into what, for you, is an ethical stance.

Level One: Self-interest

The focus is on self-gratification, preferably through mutual satisfaction, but with the intent to avoid negative personal consequences.

Level One Questions:

➤ How will I benefit?

➤ What is the quid pro quo; what will I get in return?

Level Two: System Maintenance

The intent is to maintain social order. For example, traffic laws, trash recycling, and pure-food standards are typically judged worthy of support.

Level Two Questions:

➤ Where is accountability for the system working well?

➤ How will the community benefit?

Level Three: Principled Behavior

Regardless of personal sacrifice, the desire is to pursue the greatest good for the greatest number.

Level Three Questions:

➤ Do the laws, rules, and norms support inalienable rights of all human beings?

➤ What directives do I feel impelled to resist even though I may suffer painful personal consequences?

Two exemplars of Level Three thinking are Gandhi and Martin Luther King Jr. Each dedicated himself to life-affirming principles and suffered the ultimate price. In his autobiography, Gandhi's words reflect Level Three reasoning. He wrote:

> "I did not want to offend the British magistrate personally; I wanted to offer civil resistance and decided to submit without protest to the penalty of disobedience. I disregarded his order not for want of respect for lawful authority, but in obedience to the higher law of our being, the voice of conscience."

Level Three behavior is motivated by deeply felt respect for the sanctity of all life.

To Tell the Truth?

Test yourself. How would you deal with the following situation?

Imagine your job is project manager for a construction company. One day your boss calls you into his office and says: "As you know, our client arrives tomorrow to discuss progress on his plant expansion. What you may not know is that the client's monthly payments to us, which we need for staff salaries, are based on meeting milestones spelled out in our contract. Although construction is lagging, I feel certain that during the coming months we will catch up. I want you to stretch the truth during our meeting and say we are on schedule."

How would you respond to this request from your boss?

_____

_____

_____

_____

_____

_____

_____

After writing your reaction to your boss's request, think about how you might respond from the perspective of the three levels of moral reasoning.

Author's suggestions:

Level One Response—Self-Interest
"I don't want to upset the apple cart and I certainly won't contradict what you tell the client. If asked directly, I would say we are *essentially* on schedule."

Level Two Response—System Maintenance
"To be sure I would be acting within the bounds of corporate policy, I will do what you ask, but only if you give me a written directive spelling out what you want me to say."

Level Three Response—Principled Behavior
"I would say to the client: 'Before you even ask, I want you to know that we have experienced a schedule delay for the following reasons: ... Contractually, of course, it is your right to withhold payments until we are back on schedule. But we find ourselves in this paradox: We need your monthly payments to maintain adequate staffing so we can regain our monthly milestone goals. It's like the old Navy joke about the captain telling his crew that all leaves are cancelled until morale improves.'"

When you demonstrate personal and professional integrity, you build the trust of those people vulnerable to the consequences of your behavior. This means thoughtfully resisting the small temptations of everyday ambition.

Environmental Lens

The **environmental** lens examines proposals to see if they will sustain ecological systems and safeguard aesthetic settings. Focus: *Is the environmental impact positive?*

Environmental thinking ranges from living in aesthetically pleasing surroundings at one end of the spectrum to the other extreme—viability of life on our planet. To think about our global community with a purely self-interested orientation is to court disaster.

Ecologist Garrett Hardin dramatized the need for cooperative thinking with an article in *Science* magazine, "Tragedy of the Commons." He takes the name *commons* from the central pasture of old English towns.

Hardin asks you to imagine 100 farmers each grazing one cow in the commons. Some farmers realize that by adding a second or third cow, they will have an economic advantage. At some point, however, as more farmers pursue individual gain, the added grazing will not be sustainable. In time, the result will be a field of grassless mud—making losers of all farmers, their families, and the community.

It is not a stretch to appreciate the connection between the commons metaphor and cutting down trees at an unsustainable rate, or fishing for whales without restraint, or polluting the common air with gas-guzzling vehicles. Self-centered thinking is rational only for the short term. The intent of such thinking may not be evil or malicious. Often it is simply shortsighted. No one planned on smothering Los Angeles or Mexico City in foul-smelling smog or warming the earth's atmosphere in a blanket of carbon dioxide.

How should we think about making individual interests subservient to the common good? Consider at least three strategies: regulation, incentives, and community cooperation.

Regulation

When the use of shared resources is regulated fairly and the supply is sustainable, environmental protection—rather than ruin—is a reasonable expectation. The International Whaling Commission, for example, regulates how many whales may be killed each year. The commission sets a maximum level that allows the species to remain viable.

Incentives

Modest rewards can be used to help safeguard the environment. For example, to have fewer cars clog roads, incentives could include reduced tolls and faster lanes for cars carrying multiple passengers. Companies that design flexible employee hours to help smooth traffic flow could earn positive public relations.

Community Cooperation

Social psychologist David Myers relates this experience of a cooperative community plan:

> "On the Puget Sound island where I grew up, our small neighborhood shared a communal water supply. On hot summer days when the reservoir ran low, a light came on signaling our 15 families to conserve. Recognizing our responsibility to one another and feeling that our conservation really counted, the reservoir never ran dry."

If your issue and its potential solutions have an environmental impact—physically or aesthetically—how can you embrace not only your personal or corporate needs, but also the common needs of a larger community?

_____

_____

The words of Chekhov, written more than a century ago about protecting the environment, were prophetic and sobering.

> "Man has been endowed with reason and the power to create so he can add to what he's been given. But up to now he hasn't been a creator, only a destroyer. Forests keep disappearing, rivers dry up, wild life's become extinct, the climate's ruined, and the land grows poorer and uglier every day."

When considering any proposal with environmental impact, ask: How will this action contribute to a healthful, pleasing environment—one that nurtures human spirit?

Power-Political Lens

> The **power-political** lens looks at leadership to see if its influence is adequately compelling to enlist constructive support for implementation.
> Focus: *Will others be motivated to deliver what is needed?*

The dictionary definition of *political* in this context is "the process by which power and influence are exerted." The challenge this lens brings into focus is: Can you muster the influence needed to bring a sound idea to fruition? Without an adequate power base, good ideas wither. So even if a proposal is technically sound, cost-effective, ethical, and environmentally responsible, it must also have political support.

The leadership most needed in our Information Age uses power *with* rather than power *over*. You could muster this influence with your personal power, the power of your position, or cultural power.

Personal Power

The power that comes from charisma, special expertise, or networking skills is the least intrusive. It has potency only to the extent that others choose to be influenced.

Position Power

This power comes from control of resources and information. It is potent as long as employees accept as legitimate a manager's authority to reward excellent performance, penalize poor performance, and make operational decisions.

Position power works less well at home with rebellious teenagers. ("Do it because I say so, and I'm the mother!") Even at work, if position power is used arbitrarily or ineffectively, employees might disregard their direct manager and appeal to higher-level executives. They might even choose litigation or sabotage to block implementation.

Position power also takes form as *access* to people in positions of power, as in the following story, possibly embellished, about a secretary's gate-keeping power.

> No matter how persuasively and repeatedly he tried, an ad agency job applicant couldn't get past the manager's secretary. One day, to her astonishment, the young man returned, but not as a supplicant. He appeared floating outside the manager's window in a colorful balloon with an attractive sign: "Creative, resourceful copywriter seeks challenging work." (He got the job.)

Cultural Power

This power source derives from social conditioning, such as role models, mass media, advertising, and the pressure of group norms. Cultural influences can be explicitly stated: "The way we do business around here is to make the customer our first priority."

But people are influenced more by what they see. For example, if the dominant organizational culture is to hoard power at the top, a clerk will find it difficult to resolve customer complaints on the spot. And a first-line supervisor will have a tough time authorizing overtime to meet a critical schedule.

POWER INVENTORY

Think a moment about the three power sources just described as part of the power-political lens. Look to your past and consider a current issue at work, then answer the questions below.

List a time you have used personal power to influence someone toward your way of thinking. How might you use personal power for a successful outcome on a current issue?

Past:_____

_____

Current:_____

_____

List a time you have used position power to influence someone toward your way of thinking. How might you use position power for a successful outcome on a current issue?

Past:_____

_____

Current:_____

_____

List a time you have used cultural power to influence someone toward your way of thinking. How might you use cultural power for a successful outcome on a current issue?

Past:_____

_____

Current:_____

_____

Social-Psychological Lens

> The **social-psychological** lens looks at a proposal's capacity to inspire commitment, foster teamwork, and support personal and organizational development. Focus: *Will the team or group want to work on this?*

Three factors can get in the way of group effectiveness, morale, and commitment in work settings:

> ➢ **Rationalization**

> ➢ **Cognitive Dissonance**

> ➢ **GroupThink**

Let's focus on how each of these obstacles can work against social-psychological goals.

Rationalization

When a project you have worked on turns sour, the temptation is to find reasons to blame others or find excuses. Rationalization is cover-up thinking because the truth might be an embarrassment or threat. Its aim is to prop up a person's feelings of self-worth by proving to others that she is "right." Rationalization may take form as denial, distortion, or self-delusion.

The cost of not confronting the truth, in relation to thinking clearly, is high. You forgo learning. You remain stuck at the level of presenting symptoms. Non-defensive truth telling is the first step toward discovering a creative, constructive remedy.

Cognitive Dissonance

The theory of *cognitive dissonance* was developed by social psychologist Leon Festinger. He observed that most people feel tension (*dissonance*) when two beliefs (*cognitions*) are in conflict. He concluded that to reduce the unpleasant feeling, most people adjust their thinking.

For example, when Marie submits a proposal, she expects that, as in the past, her firm will be awarded a contract. But when she learns another company has been selected, she tries to minimize the tension between her expectation and the reality by telling her manager: "I'm sure the new buyer didn't appreciate our long history together," or "The deadline for submitting a really solid proposal was unrealistically tight."

GroupThink

Thinking gets distorted when groups are so cohesive they reject views that deviate from what appears to be a consensus. Social psychologist Irving Janus called this lock-step thinking *GroupThink*.

Groups experiencing GroupThink lock into a course of action before adequately exploring alternatives. They pressure members who challenge the group idea, and they pay a heavy price to maintain team harmony.

During the Vietnam War, President Lyndon Johnson's Tuesday Lunch Group was a striking example of people clinging tenaciously to an idea to uphold the aura of group harmony. Each week the group maintained its position that aerial bombing in Vietnam coupled with defoliation and search-and-destroy missions would bring peace. This was in the face of contrary views from almost every intelligence expert and nearly all U.S. allies.

To overcome dysfunctional loyalty to premature group agreement, team members should:

➤ Encourage expression of opposing views

➤ Delay converging too quickly on a consensual solution

➤ Divide the group occasionally and reconvene to reexamine fresh thinking

➤ Invite critiques from persons with an outside perspective

➤ Convene a "second chance" meeting to air lingering doubts

For group deliberation to reflect collective wisdom, members need the freedom, support, and encouragement to speak with total candor.

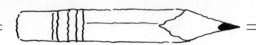

FOSTERING TEAMWORK

Think about your focal issue from the book's introduction as you complete the following exercise. Look at your issue through the social-psychological lens and write what measures you will take to minimize the three factors that get in the way of group effectiveness, morale, and commitment.

Rationalization:

What measures will you take to minimize blaming and making excuses?

_____

_____

_____

Cognitive Dissonance:

How will you encourage group members to take a realistic look at differences between expectations and reality that may crop up?

_____

_____

_____

GroupThink:

How will you support group members in speaking freely and candidly?

_____

_____

_____

4

Putting Plans

into Action

" *Never doubt that a small group of thoughtful, committed people can change the world; indeed it is the only thing that ever has.*"

–Margaret Mead

Determining a Decision-Making Strategy

After you have thought through a problem or opportunity and considered various action possibilities, how will you reach a decision when others are involved? How will you engage others in a decision whose outcome affects them? To think clearly about these questions, first you need to discriminate between strategy and process.

A decision-making *strategy* articulates *intention*—goals and values—and defines *constraints*—resources, time, level of interpersonal skill among potential decision-makers, and need for confidentiality. A strategy works when it yields an intended outcome in a timely and cost-effective manner and is accepted by the people whose energy is needed for implementation. Strategy dictates how a decision will be made and launches the actual decision-making process.

A decision-making *process* is movement along a path—gathering relevant information, examining assumptions, generating and testing alternatives, analyzing risk exposure, choosing an action plan, determining how to monitor progress, evaluating results, and learning from each experience.

Typically, people move ahead with the decision-making process before explicitly thinking about strategy. To think strategically requires understanding the four decision-making possibilities: unilateral judgment, bargaining, collaboration, and deciding-by-rule.

Unilateral Judgment

Unilateral decision-making is based on individual judgment. This strategy doesn't imply operating in isolation. Instead, unilateral decisions typically are made after others have been consulted or surveyed. In a courtroom, for example, the judge makes a unilateral decision after hearing arguments presented in adversarial debate. Whether considering a legal issue or work project, if those involved believe a unilateral decision is unfair, too costly, or simply wrong, they usually have recourse to an appeals process.

The purpose of unilateral decision-making is not to force your views down someone's throat. Its value lies in quick resolution of minor issues, such as choosing the type of staple remover; handling crises that demand immediate action, such as reacting to a bomb threat; and enforcing reasonable rules, such as requiring safety glasses.

If you *overuse* unilateral decision-making, ask yourself: Do I have an excessive need to control? Am I underestimating the competence of others? Do I, or does my organization, provide adequate staff training, coaching, and mentoring?

If you *neglect* the unilateral strategy, are you unwilling to assume responsibility for the consequences of your judgment?

A widespread problem with unilateral decision-making is getting frank input when the others' views differ from your own. In the case of a commercial airplane that had a near-collision from the pilot misreading his altimeter by 1,000 feet, the co-pilot later reported: "Even though I saw the error, I was reluctant to correct the captain." This behavior is not an isolated occurrence. Reluctance to challenge pilot judgment is common enough to be dubbed "captain-itis."

Bilateral Bargaining

A successful bargaining strategy results in a compromise between two parties that decide what each will give and receive. A decision is reached during the give-and-take of mutual adjustment when one party accepts the other's offer. The agreement reflects each party's perception of the best available outcome—in view of the power relationship—as each attempts to maximize gains and minimize concessions.

Bargaining is an appropriate decision strategy when both parties can benefit more together than either could alone. It is a *mixed motive* strategy. Participants must first *cooperate* to determine if an area of mutual benefit exists, and then *compete* to win the best deal within that area.

If you *overuse* bargaining, others may distort their needs, for example by arguing for an inflated budget request or an excessively long delivery date, expecting to be "bargained down." If you *neglect* bargaining, you might be missing opportunities to find mutually beneficial middle ground.

Effective bargaining tactics include:

➤ *Minimizing your level of authority.* Paradoxically, the more authority you are perceived to have, the less your bargaining power. Thus, it is helpful to have a buffer between you and the person with power to make a final offer. This is why car salespeople say a manager must approve the deal.

➤ *Giving concessions grudgingly.* Unless the other party believes a deal is the best you can offer, he or she may, on later reflection, decide to back out.

➤ *Seeing from the other person's perspective.* Learn what you can about what really matters to the other party so you don't give away more than you have to.

Collaboration

Collaborative decision-making aims at creative win-win solutions acceptable to all participants. Participating decision-makers must share a common purpose and values, listen well, and disclose relevant information, even when it makes them feel vulnerable. Thus, successful collaboration requires mutual trust and respect. Keep group size small enough for active discussion and large enough to include people with diverse views.

Although collaboration is the most time-consuming of the four strategies, it has offsetting benefits. Interpersonal skills are honed, teamwork is fostered, multiple perspectives are gained, and creativity is stimulated. Participants also acquire such an intimate, hands-on knowledge of the issues that decision implementation moves quickly. Unanimity is desirable but not essential as long as participants accept group decisions as worthy of energetic support.

Pitfalls include the tendency to waste time on trivial issues and to suffer through lengthy monologues by people seeking attention. As previously discussed, *GroupThink*—going along with the majority without voicing disagreement in order to appear loyal to the group—is another too-common dysfunction of collaborative decision-making. Just as unilateral decision-making can be abused by overbearing individuals, collaboration can be abused by a dominating majority.

If you *overuse* collaboration at work, you might spend too much time at meetings. If you *neglect* collaboration, you might miss opportunities for creative problem solving and for developing satisfying and productive relationships.

Decide-by-Rule (Using Objective Criteria)

Deciding-by-rule is an impersonal strategy. Participants agree in advance, using one of the other three strategies, on a clear, unambiguous rule or criterion they will accept as the basis for reaching a decision. Common decision criteria are voting, lottery, seniority, coin toss, policy statement, formula, test scores, and arbitration.

This strategy is fast, generally perceived as fair, and useful when any action is better than inaction, such as when selecting a date for a company picnic or choosing a person to work overtime during the holiday. But a decision rule, particularly voting, is rarely appropriate when the concerns of a minority of participants would benefit from full and frank discussion.

Because deciding-by-rule is impersonal, its *overuse* in decision-making would suggest a desire to avoid the friction of face-to-face confrontation. *Neglect* of this strategy, on the other hand, might be seen as a desire to be so personally involved as to be intrusive.

Variations in deciding-by-rule include multiple rounds of voting in which members receive a summary of anonymous comments from each previous round, generally concluding with round three. The best-known application of this method is the annual Academy Awards for motion pictures.

Choosing Among Strategies

In general, a decision-making strategy should be chosen that keeps costs in line with the benefits likely to accrue from a decision. Too often just the opposite occurs.

This observation led the British professor and author C. Northcote Parkinson to pen his satiric Law of Triviality: "Time spent in group deliberation on any agenda item is in inverse proportion to the cost involved." He based this "law" on his assertion that executive boards seemed to devote more time to selecting carpet color for their headquarters lobby than in reviewing long-range marketing plans.

Determining the appropriate decision-making strategy for a given situation is based on two questions as illustrated below in graphical form:

➤ Is power to be retained or shared?

➤ How well aligned are interests of the decision-makers?

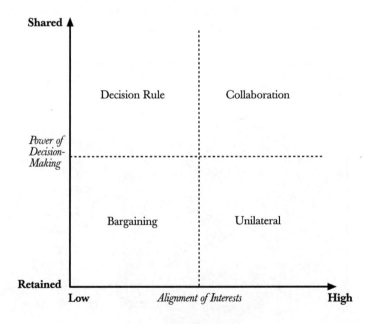

Kindler's Power/Alignment Model of Decision-Making Strategies

SALARY DECISIONS

To gain practice using the decision-making model in organizational situations, apply the diagram to the following scenario:

Imagine you manage seven people who operate independently of one another. It is salary review time. You have a fixed budget allocated for annual salary increases based on employee performance. Your own salary increases come from a different budget. The common requirement of those who report to you is creativity and other qualities that cannot be measured objectively.

Which of the four strategies is most appropriate for deciding how large a merit increase, if any, each of your direct reports will receive during the current compensation review period?

❑ Unilateral   ❑ Collaboration

❑ Bargaining   ❑ Decision-by-Rule

Why did you choose this strategy?

_____

_____

_____

_____

Author's suggestions:

➤ **Alignment.** If your staff believes you have no reason to play favorites, and if you are regarded as competent in making performance assessments—if you are trusted and respected—*alignment* will be high. You want to be fair, which is likely what your staff wants too.

➤ **Power.** Your position power is a start to getting your judgment accepted. When coupled with the power of your expertise—thoughtfully gathering relevant data, conducting open-minded performance review interviews, and protecting confidential compensation information—the legitimacy of your authority is likely to be accepted.

➤ **Strategy.** High alignment of interests, coupled with your position and personal power suggests that *retaining* your position power is appropriate.

From this reasoning, Kindler's Power/Alignment Model suggests a *unilateral* decision strategy.

MAKING MORE DECISIONS

Gain further practice using the Power/Alignment Model as you determine the most appropriate decision-making strategy in each of the following situations. Choose from:

➤ **Unilateral**   ➤ **Collaboration**

➤ **Bargaining**   ➤ **Decide-by-Rule**

1. You cannot return to your office building after the weekend earthquake until repairs take place. Alternative office space will be needed for at least a month while necessary repairs are done. What decision strategy is most appropriate (according to the model)?

_____

2. You and the other members of the board of directors need to choose a new executive director of the nonprofit agency. You must determine which skills and character traits are most important to look for in candidates for the position. What decision strategy is most appropriate?

_____

3. Management and union representatives are trying to agree on a new contract despite a wide difference in desired resolution terms. What decision strategy is most appropriate?

_____

4. In a singles tennis match during lunch hour, neither you nor your partner has been able to win by the necessary two games. You both want to win, but both need to shower and return to work. What decision strategy is most appropriate?

_____

Author's suggestions:

1. **Unilateral**: Let the CEO or general manager decide—high alignment/manager exercises retained power.

2. **Collaboration**: You and your fellow board members confer on the range of skills and traits to look for—high alignment/shared power among board members.

3. **Bargaining**: Classic situation—low alignment/each side exercises power.

4. **Decide-by-Rule**: Use a tie-breaker rule—low alignment (only one player can win)/shared power of equals.

Note: Realize that the Power/Alignment Model is only a tool. You can't turn a crank and get the "right" answer. Your judgment is what counts, so the diagram points you in a fruitful direction for choosing an appropriate decision strategy.

Implementing Decisions

Implementation, the process by which change is carried out, expresses your thinking in concrete form. The following list reviews the points you have covered so far in this book.

You are ready to realize your vision once you have:

➤ Opened your mind to the kind of change needed

➤ Accessed your creativity and inner wisdom

➤ Analyzed possibilities and risks

➤ Discussed alternatives in dialogue with others

➤ Evaluated the action plan using the six-lens criteria

➤ Selected a decision-making strategy to activate implementation

When you are ready to implement a decision, focus your thinking about the implementation process by applying the following guidelines.

WORK YOUR PLAN

Coordination

Orchestrate a logical flow of activities. For complex projects, consider regular, brief conference calls or face-to-face meetings to review progress, problems, and next steps. When in-person meetings are convened, consider stand-up gatherings in spaces without furniture to ensure brevity and focused discussion.

Contingency Planning

Anticipate "many a slip 'twixt the cup and the lip." Build an implementation schedule that accommodates misjudgment, human frailty, and changing circumstance.

Resistance

Even when people affected by change have been consulted and their needs respectfully addressed, resistance is a common expression of their discomfort with something new. Check your power base to ensure support for staying the course in the face of reactive resistance. Implementing in stages, or on a limited pilot scale, may reduce resistance.

Monitoring

Get agreement on performance standards for measuring progress at milestone intervals.

Feedback

Use follow-up interviews and surveys to gain information helpful in designing future projects.

RESOLVE YOUR ISSUE

Consider an issue or project at work that needs resolving. Use the following four points as a guide in defining an implementation process to resolve the issue.

Coordination: What is your plan for periodic team coordination during the implementation phase of your project?

_____

_____

Contingency planning: What is your "Plan B" if unforeseen circumstances disrupt constructive progress?

_____

_____

Resistance: How will you handle resistance, should it develop, to the changes you intend to implement?

_____

_____

Monitoring: How will you know that progress is adequate, and in accordance with agreed-upon performance standards?

_____

_____

Feedback: How will you get accurate, candid feedback from the implementation experience?

_____

_____

In summary, clear thinking about implementation comes into focus as a coordinated sequence of activities, a sensitivity to resistance, flexibility to meet changing circumstances, and feedback-based learning.

Learning from Your Experiences

Everyone has a limitless capacity to learn. Learning has little to do with age or seniority and everything to do with an inquiring mind and compassionate heart. People holding the same job for 20 years, who repeat their first year's experience 20 times, will have learned less than those with shorter tenure. And they will have less to contribute than those who question, probe, challenge, sift, test, and push the boundaries of how-we-do-things-around-here.

Following are common obstacles to learning. Check (✔) the ones that have held you back.

❑ Pursuing "looking good" at the expense of learning

❑ Feeling overwhelmed by other priorities

❑ Accepting conventional wisdom without testing its validity against your own experience

❑ Allowing a constant whirl of activity and busyness to preclude time for daily reflection and inquiry

❑ Declining to ask for help

❑ Assuming you already have the right answers without allowing for not knowing

❑ Letting yourself be flooded with feelings or deluged with data

❑ Disregarding your gut feelings and your intuitive insights

❑ Declining to review your thinking with coaches, mentors, and other independent thinkers

These are obstacles you can overcome with thoughtful attention and practice.

> Outstanding performance depends on
> thinkers who see what is so,
> imagine what is possible, and
> find ways to bridge the gap.

OVERCOMING OBSTACLES

Review the items in the checklist on the previous page and select up to three of those you checked. For each one, describe an example of how that obstacle has held you back when you have wanted to pursue a new experience. Then write a way you could work to overcome this obstacle.

Obstacle: _____

This obstacle has held me back in my pursuit of: _____

_____

_____

I can work to overcome this obstacle by: _____

_____

_____

Obstacle: _____

This obstacle has held me back in my pursuit of: _____

_____

_____

I can work to overcome this obstacle by: _____

_____

_____

Obstacle: _____

This obstacle has held me back in my pursuit of: _____

_____

_____

I can work to overcome this obstacle by: _____

_____

_____

Translating Your Thinking into Action

Create an action plan for the central issue you identified in the introduction. Use the following questions as a springboard.

1. Identify the work or personal issue you want to clarify.

_____

_____

_____

2. What is the larger system of which this issue is one component part?

_____

_____

_____

3. What are one or more incremental refinements that would improve the system in which your issue is currently embedded? Are these adequate? For how long?

_____

_____

_____

_____

_____

4. What is a radical new approach that would transform the current system? Whether a problem or an opportunity, transforming the current system will open fresh resolution possibilities.

_____

_____

_____

_____

_____